Journey...

From Darkness to Light

Jeanne Buesser

Author, He Talks Funny

Moonlight Till Dawn

Dedicated to my parents,

Renée and Carl Schlesinger

Index

PROLOGUE

My journey... where do I begin? How did I get here? How have I survived this far? I can tell you that I don't know. The journey began the day I was born: a six month preemie weighing 2lb 2oz, twelve inches long, the size of a small game hen. My mom told me I wasn't expected to live. God must have had other plans for me.

Fast forward ...

From ages six until thirteen years old, I lived in East Africa with my family. My dad's opportunity to build a printing school brought us there and we lived well. When I returned to the United States in junior high, this "new kid on the block" struggled academically but with hard work, I made it through. After graduating high school, and a few years of work, I found the right man, Ray Buesser, and I fell in love. We were married with dreams of the happy family in our future. Dreams don't always become reality.

First, Ray's older brother was diagnosed with leukemia. Ray served as his brother's bone marrow replacement donor as part of a treatment regimen offered in the state of Washington. He spent two months away from home and I spent lonely nights crocheting a queen-size afghan for our bed.

Later, when Ray's brother's treatment didn't work, Ray was called upon again to donate his platelets. That treatment succeeded and his brother is alive and well. Soon after, we had our first son, Danny, and I learned how to love someone more than anyone else in the world. Danny was active, happy and energetic. When Danny was 2 ½, he was joined by a younger sibling, Adam. Now a family of four, life seemed good.

A year later we dealt with the unthinkable. Our beloved son, Danny, died from a rare cancerous abdominal tumor. He deteriorated within twenty-four hours of diagnosis. As parents, we reeled in shock. How could this happen? We were told that this rare disease progressed from its onset to becoming life-threatening within six weeks. He had presented with few symptoms. I remember little before the funeral. I do recall telling the family doctor that my husband needed medication to help him calm down before the funeral. Ray was despondent.

I don't remember much of anything else. Eating, sleeping, and running errands occupied my time. Time passed in such a blur, I honestly don't recall events of that entire first year. Raising a younger son, Adam, a thirteen-month old quiet baby, became rote. I do remember shortly after the funeral wanting to tell people in the supermarket that I had lost a son, and expected understanding and support from total strangers.

Ten days after Danny's death, I found some solace. I attended my first meeting of the Compassionate Friends support group, comprised of bereaved parents. However, that too remains a blur. I found that serving as the chapter librarian and helping with a Children's Memorial Day event kept me involved and gave me something to do. Each day, every week and month without Danny passed slowly and painfully. Suddenly, one day I decided I couldn't go back to "that place," the very beginning for the newly bereaved. I wasn't there anymore, I had moved on.

For sympathy whenever I needed it, there were my cats. A loving line of special felines: Mitzy, Mittens, Mistletoe, Tony, Frazzle and Anya. My cat companions, before and after I was married, listened to me talk and cry. On my bed or on my lap, Mistletoe helped to release my feelings. There have always been cats in my life.

Ray handled his grief differently. He went to work every day. He didn't mention Danny. Compassionate Friends and other support groups didn't interest him. At some point I started writing poetry. That undertaking served as therapy for me.

After several miscarriages, I became pregnant again with Josh, and our family became four, instead of the five that we should have been. One of the hardest things was most people never mentioned our fifth member, Danny. He was always present in my mind. Milestones arrived and passed and for most folks, it was another day. How hard it was on me as his brothers passed their 4th birthdays. Danny died before celebrating his.

What made it especially hard was that approaching age 4, Adam, my second son (the quiet one), was diagnosed with a severe speech disorder called Apraxia. Still a bereaved parent, I tried to focus on his needs. Adam wasn't verbal at the time. He had appointments with doctors and therapists and other professionals.

I took him to all of them, trying to cope with this new challenge while I still missed Danny, every day.

Josh was another story. He also wasn't developing the same way that Danny had. At age 20 months he was diagnosed with PDD-NOS a condition on the Autism Spectrum. This was a new bump in the road, a detour on my journey, one which allowed me to learn to advocate for my two younger sons.

Time marches on and then, like Danny, my husband passed away without warning. Another tragedy seared through me, making me relive some of the grief of Danny's death.

My sisters proved a God-send, helping me put my affairs in order and helping me to organize things during that awful time. Because it was so hard to know how to deal with all the twists and turns including all of the care and attention that Adam and Josh needed, I started going to grief therapy.

I realized that I had carried around the grief for Danny so long that I no longer knew what it was to live again as me. There were many things that I hadn't talked about for so long. I died inside when Danny died and I was just going through the motions of being a mom to my kids. I started to work to achieve a more positive attitude, and embrace life one day at a time.

Grief had become so comfortable for me that I didn't know anything else, and did not feel overly depressed but I learned that I must emotionally and psychologically grow in a better direction for my remaining children. Starting over left me scared. To receive help you must first want to access the help that is out there.

I read a lot. I read books on grief. I read poetry. It is one thing to read a poem that inspires and another to actually act on its meaning:

Ascension

And if I go,
while you're still here...
Know that I live on,
vibrating to a different measure
--behind a thin veil you cannot see through.
You will not see me,
so you must have faith.
I wait for the time when we can soar together again,
--both aware of each other.
Until then, live your life to its fullest.
And when you need me,
Just whisper my name in your heart,
...I will be there.

Used with Author's Permission. Ascension ©1987 by Colleen Corah Hitchcock, 1031 W. Indian Hills Pl., Phoenix, AZ 85023. Colleen Hitchcock is the author of *Rabbit Heart* (Simon & Schuster) her web site is: www.colleenhitchcock.com.

Others ask me how to do this. I tell them, "Live your life to the fullest though loved ones in your family have left this life." As difficult as continuing this journey feels, I haven't yet faced the hardest part, making real change. I continue to write poetry for each event or milestone. I never forget Danny and always wonder what he would look like or sound like now.

Ray and I continued to raise our children through the challenge of our individual bereavements. At this stage, I can look back and understand the frustration in my husband's outlook as we raised our boys with special needs.

Where are we today? The boys are in middle school and high school; both students on the honor roll. I am so proud of them. We try to enjoy each day.

I often reflect on how the sudden death of my husband left me raising my kids Adam and Josh with little emotional and physical support. I do still have many times when long-buried feelings resurface. I have begun to go back to the blur of that year after Danny died and remember how I felt.

Adam and Josh and I have survived a year and a half since Ray's death. I've tried some new ways to help myself heal. I was surprised to find that Tai' Chi Chuh lessons really help me focus on spiritual energy. I really try to find positive energy or that special place inside me first.

I know that I can make a difference. I've tried to take stock of what I have accomplished.I've realized that in order to make a difference in this world and to contribute, you have to work hard and continue moving ahead on your journey, even when you can't see what's ahead.

I've taken some steps in these past few years that I never thought I could. I wrote a few articles for magazines on Apraxia and some about parenting my kids. One of them I titled, Going From Darkness to Light. In hindsight, I didn't realize that the title describes my journey.

One of the first positive steps after Ray's death which I took was to accomplish one dream of mine, self publishing a book on Apraxia awareness. It feels really good to have done that.

I have realized that you have to re-invent yourself, take risks, try new things and evolve like a butterfly emerging from its cocoon. You have changed. I learned that I cannot carry the ball alone. I need backup, resources, support, friends you really can count on, and family otherwise I'll burn out fast.

Spiritually speaking, I have found that it is okay to ask God or your guardian angel for help and direction through prayer. Many times I don't know how to initiate change, or *how to reach a desired destination but I now have the faith that it will come. I have learned, too, that raising teenagers alone isn't easy, and raising two who have special needs means I must find even more strength.*

Taking it one day at a time helps. I no longer pressure myself or am no longer so hard on myself. I am not perfect and all I can do is give my best. I will make mistakes, but that's okay. I know that whatever energy expended, negative or positive, comes back to you threefold. Sometimes you live only for your kids and forget about yourself.

I learned that some family relationships cannot be changed. I can't make people talk about their memories of Danny, or make them continue to reach out to me when they choose not to. Now with Ray gone, for some people, I'm back to square one. They don't want to talk about the dead, even when their memories of better times could help me and the kids.

Being a widow is really difficult. I realize that I have to do things by myself, I don't have a spouse for backup.

It has been hard learning to laugh again and to enjoy life but I'm finding new friends. It is something I need to do. So many people encourage me to publish my poems. I need to tell people of my journey, how I made it to a brighter side. I am still is a work in progress.... I am not afraid to say that.

I want to thank my family, parents, sisters, and special friends, (old and new), who have helped and supported me on this journey. To the people who have passed on, who watch over me. To Jenna, for building my websites. My wish is may you all have inner peace and healing light.

Jeanne Hope Schlesinger Buesser

www.JeanneBuesser.com
http://health.groups.yahoo.com/group/ApraxiaNetwork/
http://parentsptofview.blogspot.com
http://Authorsden.com

Poems

To Danny, Moving On – Part 1 - 10/15/97

Life is like an ocean wave, neither stopping, nor slowing.

Sometimes you wish, just once, to hold a moment in time.

But the waves continue to crash, beating down on the shore.

You left us way before your time. It is hard going on

without you, my son.

You'll never grow older, but forever stay young in my

heart and mind.

To Danny, Moving On – Part II - 6/14/99

Danny, you were my little lion.

When you roared they heard you down the hall.

Now Adam's passed your age and is growing so tall. His

birthday's almost here. You never made it to 4.

It will be hard for me, I miss you more and more.

I look for you when Adam's playing.

Joshua's eldest brother you'll always be.

I can't kiss or read to you at night. Tears flow.

Life goes on and we all grow older.

You're up in heaven and we're here below.

Halloween - 10/26/97

Halloween approaches and you're not here.

I remember holding your hand, ringing the bells as we
walked along.

Do you have Halloween in heaven?

I know you're an angel going here and there, my son,
happier now, not in pain. You live in my heart again.

Hanukkah - 12/18/97

Danny, the lights shine less brightly since you're not
here to light them.

With the lighting of the candles, I miss your face and
smile.

Nearly five now, I'll wonder what you look like.

You visited me last year at Hanukkah.

Could you come again?

It gets harder going on. The energy I had is gone.

Days are just the same, something lost and not re-
gained.

My Card - 1/27/99

There is a card I'm waiting for from you to me, you see.

A little heart, a sign that says you still love me.

I know I'm asking for something heaven sent.

I miss you so much it hurts and that is what I meant.

Another year and holiday has come and gone.

I look towards the door.

I wipe a tear and remember it as it was before.

The Sailboat - 9/5/99

On the sailboat a captain hoists the sail.

Sailing the seas,

He knows not where he goes.

His first mate a young boy, laughing.

Wind blows through their hair.

One day I will join them on their voyage.

Until then I will wait for them to call me home.

Your 3rd Anniversary - 8/18/99

How can I hold on knowing the day is coming near?

A new year is almost here.

The day you died is as it was three years ago.

I'm going through the paces without splitting at the seams.

I will never forget, the day you died, it is fresh as yesterday.

I need your strength once more Danny, as I go out the door to shul.

For Danny - 6/12/00

In my heart and mind you'll always be

never far away from me.

You're hope and strength when there is none.

You give me light, my first born son.

When I'm sad and in despair,

somehow I hope you're always there.

Danny, don't be mistaken, I love Adam & Josh, too.

They're not you.

This year is the hardest you see

you're gone more years than alive from me.

So when my time to go is near,

I'll not be scared or full of fear.

You'll come to guide me home,

I'll never again be alone.

Lighting the Hannukah Candle - To Danny 11/25/00

How quickly the holidays approach. Hanukkah is
almost here.

I remember five years ago your looking at the candles
and lighting them.

Even though you're not here to light it, the flame is
always lit in my heart,

Fueled by my love.

The Mall - 8/01

Two fathers/husbands meet, both bereaved parents, not knowing what to expect of the other. Each had asked questions about the other spouse. Only the wives had met and become good friends. Both of them greet each other.

The two fathers thought the same thoughts, talked and acted as though twins. Maybe they were brothers in another life? Each hurt but didn't know what to say about their loved one. Each

child had surviving siblings. They talked, but there was a shared silence of knowing that something was missing. One ached because it was too painful to talk about a missing son, even with their spouse.

The wives laughed and continuing through down the mall while the husbands shared a glance. All exchanged goodbyes and went their separate ways.

Fathers/husbands are supposed to provide for their families holding everyone together. Talking to a spouse presents a different story. Each has his own silence on how life has changed.

Our lost children remain in spirit, in our hearts forever. All grieve differently.

To All the Survivors of the World Trade Center -
9/11/01

Where do I start? Your world spins in sudden turmoil.

You're a passenger on a sailboat in a stormy ocean at

the mercy of swells, your lives changed forever.

Strangers among you share a common bond. Find

comfort among them. They'll be a newly extended family

and friends.

Support each other. Don't blame yourselves. Know this,

That wherever you are your loved one's spirit will be.

Speak of them often.

Write down memories. Know they are safe inside your

hearts and minds.

*Dedicated in memory of Daniel Scott Buesser's 5th
anniversary of his passing (9/11/96)*

A Change of Seasons - 11/15/01

The air feels colder, a change of season leaves begin to fall.

Leaves change color, days grow shorter.

I remember your playing in the leaves.

Was it so long ago? Only 5 years have passed.

Turning 40 this year has been hard.

Outside I tie my coat a little tighter.

I'm trying to keep warm while watching your brothers play,

Knowing somewhere you're out there. There will always be a change of seasons.

Your Spirit - 4/29/02

Though I cannot see nor touch it, your spirit is always

with me.

You keep me going when I lose strength to go on.

It is hard now.

Josh will have outlived you after your birthday.

How my heart aches, I look to you for guidance.

This new road I travel has no map or directions,

I know you will lead me to learn life's lessons.

Thank you for being my help and my son.

The Empty Chair - 9/4/02

On Danny's 6th Anniversary

There is always an empty chair.

Where you should be sitting, my son.

I wish I could see you grow. You'd be 9 3/4 years now.

I wonder where you are, I'm sure you've been busy

up in heaven and reside beyond a distant star.

Just thought I'd let you know I think of you

sometimes.

To Danny - 11/17/02

Through the forest your spirit walks down the path to
where we are.

A picture hangs on the wall.

Love knows no distance nor boundaries.

I only wish for you to gain more knowledge in your
journey as you go on now.

So we light the candles and put up the tree wishing that
you stood near.

Another year's ending, a new one begins.

Give us strength as your 10th birthday approaches.

With silent tears we miss you.

Winter Puzzle - 12/02

It is cold outside and dark.

The wind blows fiercely. My body prepares itself for a long winter.

I bought a 1000 piece puzzle after you died. It shows two cats looking outside a curtained window at two cardinals on a snow- laden tree.

One day I will get enough nerve to start and finish it. The puzzle shows me that even in the bleakest days of winter, there is beauty if you just look.

How interesting that even a puzzle can warm you heart and give you hope for another day.

Snow - 12/9/02

Falling snow so beautiful to see,

A memory comes back. You're nearly three,

pulling your baby brother in a sled. You pull too hard.

Adam too surprised to cry, just lays there in the snow.

You push him up again. He's ready to go.

You look down from heaven now as Josh and Adam play.

The snow is melting. The memory sadly fades away.

Spring - 3/16/03

The warm sun melts winter ice and snow. Water flows

everywhere.

Birds sing, the sky is blue.

Children splash and jump in puddles. I think of you.

As the water recedes, small green shoots will emerge

from frozen ground.

They make no sound. Flowers will once more bloom,

showing me spring is here.

Passover Faces (friends and relatives) - 3/17/03

We gather at the table, and sip the wine,

We talk about our heritage, what happened

in the past.

Some one fills Elijah's cup, and opens the door.

Sadly I remember faces that aren't here anymore.

I remember horseradish sandwiches, and Matzoh Brei.

I look at empty chairs. They stare back.

RAINBOW - 4/6/03

The sky was cold and cloudy,

Grim clouds a murky gray

I miss you.

A storm came up fast.

Wind kicked up and rain

started to come down.

We all went inside.

It lasted three minutes.

We returned outside.

Gray swirling clouds moved over the house.

A small patch of blue appeared far in the distance.

My younger son said look.

I turned around to see a small rainbow.

Quick as a wink it came and went.

Thanks Danny!

The Butterfly - 4/24/03

What is a butterfly but a beautiful, delicate fragile insect seen in the spring. It is also a unique-many colored creature varying in size fluttering its wings progressively going from flower to flower.

Each day, braving uncertain fate, but forging on. It emerges slowly from its safe cocoon into an unsure world.

Like the butterfly, bereaved parents, rise up, stretch our wings and face a new day. Each butterfly renews itself differently. We are not the same, but each is beautiful in his own way. Our children, like the butterflies, remind us of life's innocence, grace and wonder.

Colors of Your Rainbow - 4/30/03

What are the colors of your rainbow?

Yellow, warmth of sunshine?

Orange, peaceful sunset?

Red, the beauty in a rose?

Blue, the ocean's depth?

Violet, the patience of a growing flower?

Green, the serenity of inner peace and health?

Though everyone's colors show different hues and

meaning, they blend together. Each one of us is unique

and special.

Colors of the rainbow lift our spirits towards the sky.

What is a Poem?

What is a poem but words on a page?

You write them down hoping that

people understand.

Are you sad, happy, hopeful, full of rage?

Did you ask someone to take your hand, to help you

walk them thru this pain?

How do I start again?

Just words upon a page.

A blank page at first, then words start to flow.

How many changes? No one ever knows. They're only

words you see.

Until my thoughts start again, another page by me.

A Summer Storm - 8/2003

A newly bereaved member told his story last night in the group,

I was reminded of how I felt nearly 8 years ago.

Picture a summer storm with fierce, relentless wind,

Whipping rain and dangerous lightning. You are a tree barely holding on as the storm take its toll on your body. Emotions are tossed around. Lightning strikes you acquire a new wound.

Your body reels and cannot hold its ground.

Slowly the storm subsides and you are left trying to stand.

Slowly, very slowly you begin to take baby steps and lifting up your badly bruised body.

It will take a long time but like that tree you will always bear that wound. Someday you will grow roots and branches. There is always the possibility that the storm will return.

There was a Time - 11/30/03

There was a time not so long ago, you were here, playing in the snow, making snow balls and snowmen in the yard.

Another year gone.

Faded memories hard to retrieve It's been 8 years now, Hard to believe, your smile, your voice, not seen nor heard.

As the candles are lit, I say a prayer you're always there in my heart.

Your brothers grow up, without you here.

Spring - 5/04

Ahhhh, the first day of spring. What a beautiful day! It looks delightful from inside the house. Beware, Old Man Winter wants to keep his rule!

Cold wind whips around corners chilling tulips emerging from the frozen ground.

Mother Nature tries to warm the earth, but is having a hard time of it.

Like the season, a bereaved parent can't predict the weather looking from inside the house. Each of us tries to cope again after a cold winter.

Hope - 5/2/04

What is it? A distant memory?

Hope is more than a feeling of dreams

not yet reached.

It is support given to friends and family

that show you care.

Hope gives you strength to look ahead. Even in the

darkest moments and days.

The Fall - 10/09/04

The weather is changing, leaves turn different colors .

They fall as the wind blows, rustling beneath your feet.

It has been eight years, Danny.

A distant faded memory you were so young, playing in

the leaves.

I'm afraid to lose the few memories. I miss hearing your

voice and seeing your face. I'm glad I had you though,

you taught me how to live and love.

Thanksgiving - 11/11/04

The food is cooking, the table

is almost set,

Guests will soon be here.

I look around and sigh, missing you,

wishing you were here.

Some other people are missing,

They also cannot be seen,

They're thought of, lovingly in spirit, in our hearts.

Before we sit down to eat, I'll send you

a wish too. "May you always be in white light,

the journey an easy learning experience for you".

Know that you can visit me in dreams anytime. You

wait in a different place among rainbow beams.

Another Birthday - 1/25/05

Another birthday Danny...

2004 has come and gone,

Your birthday just passed to.

Sometimes when I think of you,

I wonder where I'm going.

This road called life has cracks and bumps

which make you stumble, climb and fall.

Sometimes you have nothing to hold on to,

like your back is against a wall.

What lessons I've learned my son, are these, so far

No one can tell you what to do. You learn by doing.

No one can take that away from you.

So thank you for helping and teaching me by showing

the way.

I know that you and others guide me along the

path. Happy 12th Birthday!

Dreams

What are dreams?

Are they things we wished we had achieved?

Are they reminders of things that we have yet to do?

Are they a communication portal from earth

to where our loved ones are?

I think dreams are a constant reminder

to keep us on our toes, or to steer us in a direction.

Awaiting Spring - 3/18/05

I look around. The snow is nearly gone, a sign that

spring is coming. The sky seems softer, days grow

warmer, cardinals sing in the trees.

Soon the ground will not be frozen, flowers will emerge

from the ground. They're trying to show their colors to

the world. Once again, Mother Earth is trying to renew

herself from under a blanket of snow.

We, too, try to renew our spirits as a new season begins.

Loved ones are always around us. Sometimes in

everyday things. we forget the signs that they are here.

Mother's Day - 5/8/05

It seems so long ago I held you in my arms. You were

just a babe.

A first time mom, not sure of what or how to do things,

You held onto my finger to let me know you were there.

You grew up quickly, soon a toddler, going to nursery

school.

Your younger brother came along and you weren't sure
how to

approach that. You were 3 1/2. I tried my best to look

after you.

Then suddenly you were gone.

Now I look up to you. Thanks for being my 1st son.

The Open Door - 8/30/05

The open door that I cannot see is right here,

it stands in front of me.

I can't go through.

It is closed to me.

It is where you come to visit me.

Some day I know I'll have the key and

knowledge to go see through.

Right now it is only open to you,

my son.

My journey here is far from done.

I have to gain experience to earn the key.

November Rain - 11/16/05

The November sky looms cloudy and drizzly, a light rain

falls on my face.

It pulls me back to another time and place when you

were here playing in the rain, jumping in the puddles.

To hear your laughter again in my mind.

The leaves have turned and fallen, the wind is warm

and strong.

Thanksgiving is almost here, in my heart your spirit

lives on.

The Cardinal - 12/05/05

In the early morning after a recent fallen snow a

cardinal chirps and flies onto an evergreen tree.

How beautiful he is on a branch. His deep red coat

contrasts with the bright white snow.

Sometimes we have to awaken from the cold harshness

of winter to see the beauty that lies before us, to find

things yet un-discovered about ourselves.

Another Day - 4/15/06

Spring is here,

Flowers bloom, trees blossom.

Birds return to sing their song.

The sky is blue, the sun shines,

but something is missing, you!

Your brothers grow, but somehow I

sense they miss you.

Josh just turned 7 and released his balloons

up to you.

This year is hard.

It'll be 10 years in Sept.

Where did the time go?

I know you are busy on whatever journey you are on

and learning.

Someday I hope to make you proud of me, as I learn on

my journey here.

I'm striving to be near you in my heart.

The Stream - 7/13/06

The stream begins from an unknown source, has no

destination nor knows what danger lies ahead.

Birds, and frogs enjoy it. Fish swim in it. Fish count on

its way providing food, and protection.

Like the stream we aren't sure of knowing how we got to

where we are, or by what force we continue on.

Each day we learn new things and face new perils.

I have learned how to keep on going no matter what.

Cleansing Rain - 8/3/06

Rain cleans the leaves and feeds their roots.

Tears cleanse the soul.

Rain nourishes the needy earth.

As tears heal the soul and heal, the body replenishes

itself. Rain gives life to dry starved roots.

Sometimes we have to cry in order to grow.

Thinking - 11/28/06

Thinking of this year that's almost past,

It's hard to fathom, How fast 10 years have gone.

You're in my thoughts and prayers at night

I wish I could hold you once again and see you in my

dreams,

Your birthday's just around the bend,

It helps to know you lead me onto paths I won't dread,

You're with me always even though you can't be

touched.

That love transcends all boundaries, my son,

I thank you very much, for strengthening me to move

ahead

to another year, to know somehow that you are always

here.

The Candle - 12/7/06

We light the candles, say the prayer, sing the songs

from the heart,

Others gone are here in spirit, and we hold them.

Memories are hard to call up because over time they

fade.

Like a candle ever burning its sincere presence,

The light will not go out as long as we believe,

They always will be with us, sadly even as

we grieve.

The Light Within - 12/11/06

The light within glows from a spark so tiny no one can

See where the source is and what fuels it. It is the love

between you and me. In the darkness you've shed light

on which way to go which way is next, what I learn will

as I move.

The special friends and bonds of which you know,

How can I repay you for all you've given me? The love

you show and help me on this journey beyond the sea?

I only hope to honor you by the deeds you help me do.

No matter what ever the task, or the effort, it is all that

I can do. Because my son, you've given me more than

I can ask of you!

The Rose Bush - 2/9/07

What is a rose, but a thorny prickly bush that
grows in any old way without shape or form.
It is the flower which grows in its pod,
which we don't see that has beauty.
Dainty petals, colors inside, slowly unfold to a bud.
Morning dew glistens in its outer leaves revealing soft
colors to the world.
Like the bush, we come in different colors
and manifest different shapes. Though our
outside may appear rough the flower we produce,
reveals the true beauty that lies inside all of us. Only a
few people who really know us well can see.

The Puzzle - 6/1/07

The puzzle box is on the table,1000 pieces scattered all

around,

I put it together, many colors and shapes to be found.

Each day I struggle again to find the ones that fit.

Some days it seems hopeless, fighting myself a bit

Like a needle in a haystack, for the right pieces to finish

one more inch of this endless picture, tests my pride.

I hope to finish it soon, because I promised this to you

over 10 years ago, as I cried.

It's a tribute to all you've given me, though it is going so,

so slow.

I will make all the pieces fit, you know.

September, 2007 - 9/7/07

The school bus arrives- the kids get on.

It drives away. An empty feeling is left

Inside. I look for you in junior high school kids,

You'd be almost 15. Adam, asked me about

you yesterday, saying he missed you.

I thought I wouldn't hear those words because he

was so little when you died. My heart stopped,

I paused, didn't know what to say.

We all miss you, on your very special day, 11 years

later without your voice or face. But we know you're

always around in your special place.

Thoughts of You - 12/5/07

Snow flakes falling gently,

slowly to the ground. So pretty to

look falling without sound.

Danny, it seems so long ago, since you

were around.

I wonder how your journey's going up above,

It is so far away from here.

Yet, sometimes missing you I need your guidance near.

This path is without trails or directions almost a

journey within one's self, continuing along daily gaining

insight to follow a path.

One day I will see you in another place and time.

Until we meet again you'll always be a son of mine.

Life -12/9/07

Ocean waves rise and fall,

swell and crash on the shore.

The tide playfully teases ocean life underneath

the waves and on the sand.

The sun rises and sets.

Another day approaches. The circle of life

And death continues on.

The Sky

Gray threatening clouds have covered the sky. Any

minute it will rain, I think.

It is awfully quiet, no wind just clouds drifting gently by.

Few birds in the trees.

The world seems to pause today, unrushed just slowly

moving on.

A trace of blue appears but is quickly covered up as

more clouds appearing in the sky.

Japanese Maple Tree - 11/8/08

The day is cloudy, rainy and wet. Many trees have shed

their colored leaves, leaving only a bare shell

while others with leaves let them gracefully fall to the

ground.

Outside the window a vibrant red Japanese maple

stands out against the dreary landscape.

12 years have passed since you were here, hard to

believe.

Though our family struggles on, like the tree you show

that even in quiet days color and hope persist.

Thank you for watching over us all.

A New Milestone - 12/4/08

Today, Adam picked out his tallit.

As Adam approaches his bar mitzvah life is bittersweet.

You would have had yours already Danny.

You would know how to feel. It's scary.

I wish you were here.

I am so proud of Adam who tries so hard.

I know you'll be there in spirit, but I still miss you.

The Open Door ✤

You look and talk with your eyes,

They're gentle, kind, and innocent.

Sparkling, they pierce my soul.

Somehow, at sometime, I will hear your hidden voice.

You look to me for guidance. Until then, you grow and I

will wait until that door opens to hear my name.

✤ "The Open Door" - A documentary for families with speech disorders.

Teachers - 3/10/11

Teachers as friends, co-workers help us pass the days.

What we learn from what they say and do sometimes

hard to lead us onward.

Teachers, they support us and help us in this life we

lead, even if we're not strong.

They inspire and teach us important life lessons.

The Beacon - 7/2011

Light pierces the darkness showing me the say,

Waves relentlessly crash upon the rocks,

Sending spray everywhere,

The beacon doesn't waver, glowing brightly until the

dawn.

#########

Letters

9/01 - (Danny In memory of your Fifth Anniversary)

Danny,

I thought about you the other day. The sky was a beautiful shade of blue, like your eyes. I remembered you funeral, how beautiful a day it was!

I said that you'd be proud of how everything went that day. I can hardly believe it is 5 years since I saw you face, heard your voice, or read you a story at night. Adam is growing up and so is Josh. I wish sometimes you were still here to play with Adam and Josh. Adam needs and misses a big brother.

You know, on vacation we visited a child's amusement park called "Story Land" in NJ. Just for a moment, I remembered we went to the same place in Vermont, NH when you were nearly two. Thank you for the memory. We will always love & miss you.

Love,

Mommy, Daddy, Adam & Josh.

Your 12ᵗʰ Anniversary - 9/11/08

Birds chirp, bugs crawl , planes fly; the wind is still,
Missing and thinking of you today, knowing you're here,
Cool breezes gently blow, the balloon is skyward.
Thank you for being my son and watching over us all.

The Journey - 7/02

The road on this journey is rough. Sometimes I stumble
and can't get up nor want to. Some days is a question
on where I'm going? How will I get there? What is the
purpose? There are more questions them answers.

I know as I travel along this road, someone will guide
me revealing the reason for my journey. Some days I ask
myself why.

As parents we have all been to the darkest reaches of
our soul, and slowly life takes us on a different journey
to reach the same destination, going on.

The journey must be lived day by day, hour by hour. I
didn't choose this road,
I now travel it I having gained insight to the world's
perspective, being thankful for each day never taking
Anything for granted.

New friendships evolving through the connection of
shared grief from friends who support me on my
journey.

The Surprise - 7/03

The other day I was trimming my bush in the front yard. I turned around and started trimming some brown branches from my evergreen.

A beautiful white and black butterfly appeared from the bushes and fluttered in front of my face.

I thanked Danny for sending it and apologized to it because I nearly killed it with the trimmers.

Danny's 8th Year Anniversary - 9/03

I thought about you today, It was hard to believe it has been so long, without you here. How did I make it this far? I don't remember the other years went so fact all a blur. I don't remember what you sounded like, I miss your face.

I have to keep on looking at the last picture to refresh my memory. I love the card from TCF they remind me that I'm not along. Even though we all get older our children as always in our hearts.

In 2 years it will be the hardest. When Danny would have been 13, and going thru his bar mitzvah. I have always wanted to get bat mitzvahed and never did. Maybe one day I will get the courage to do it and also honor Danny too.

A Funny Story (in loving memory of Danny) - 6/5/06

The other day both of my kids were going to school. Josh, my little guy kept asking for his sandals for his feet. I had looked all over the house and outside also for them but to no avail. I also asked Adam to look too before he went to school, and asked him whether he had found them. He said no. I put sneakers on Josh's feet and went to work. What do you think I saw when I got home by the couch? Josh's sandals. I laughed and thanked Danny for finding them; I guess he wanted to play hide and seek?

##########

Resources and References

Bozarth, Alla Renee. *A Journey Through Grief.* Center City: Hazelden, 1994.

Print.

Brener, Anne. *Mourning and Mitzvah: A Guided Journal for Walking the*

Mourner's Path Through Grief. Woodstock: Jewish Lights Publishing,

1994. Print.

Fitzgerald, Helen. *The Mourning Handbook.* New York: Simon and Schuster,

1995. Print.

Fox, Sandy. *Creating a New Normal After the Death of a Child.* Bloomington:

iUniverse, Inc., 2010. Print.

Hanson, Warren. *The Next Place.* Minneapolis: Waldman House, 1997. Print.

Hickman, Martha Whitmore. *Healing After Loss, Daily Meditations of Working*

    Through Grief. New York: Avon Books, Inc., 1994. Print.

Liss, Moe. *Debbie's Stories.* New York: YBK Publishers, Inc., 2003. Print.

McCracken, Anne and Mary Semel. *A Broken Heart Still Beats After Your Child*

    Dies. Center City: Hazelden, 1998. Print.

Mellonie, Brian and Robert Ingpen. *Lifetimes.* New York: Bantam Books, 1983.

    Print.

    NJGroups.org. online database, 2000